Bad Bet

By Stephen Rickard

Published in 2026 by
Norwood House Press
2544 Clinton Street
Buffalo, NY 14224

Printed in the United States of America

Library of Congress Cataloging-in-Publication Data:
Names: Rickard, Stephen, 1957-, author. | Hawkins, Daisy, author.
Title: Bad bet / written by Stephen Rickard. Tennis / written by Daisy Hawkins.
Description: Buffalo, NY : Norwood House Press, 2026. | Series: Phonics all-stars: phase 2 |
Identifiers: ISBN 9781978577756 (pbk.) | ISBN 9781978577763 (library bound) | ISBN 9781978577770 (ebook)
Subjects: LCSH: Reading–Phonetic method–Juvenile literature. | English language–Phonetics–Juvenile literature. | Animals–Juvenile literature. | Tennis–Juvenile literature.
Classification: LCC LB1573.3 R534 2026 | DDC 372.465–dc23

CPSIA compliance information: Batch #CW26NHP: For further information contact Norwood House Press at 1-800-237-9932.

I had a bug.

The bug had a red back.

I met a big cat.

I bet the big cat can not get the bug.

I met a big dog.

I bet the big dog can not get the bug.

The big dog ran at the bug, but it did not get it.

I met a bat.

I bet the bat can not get the bug.

Bad bet!

The bat **did** get the bug.

Tennis

By Daisy Hawkins

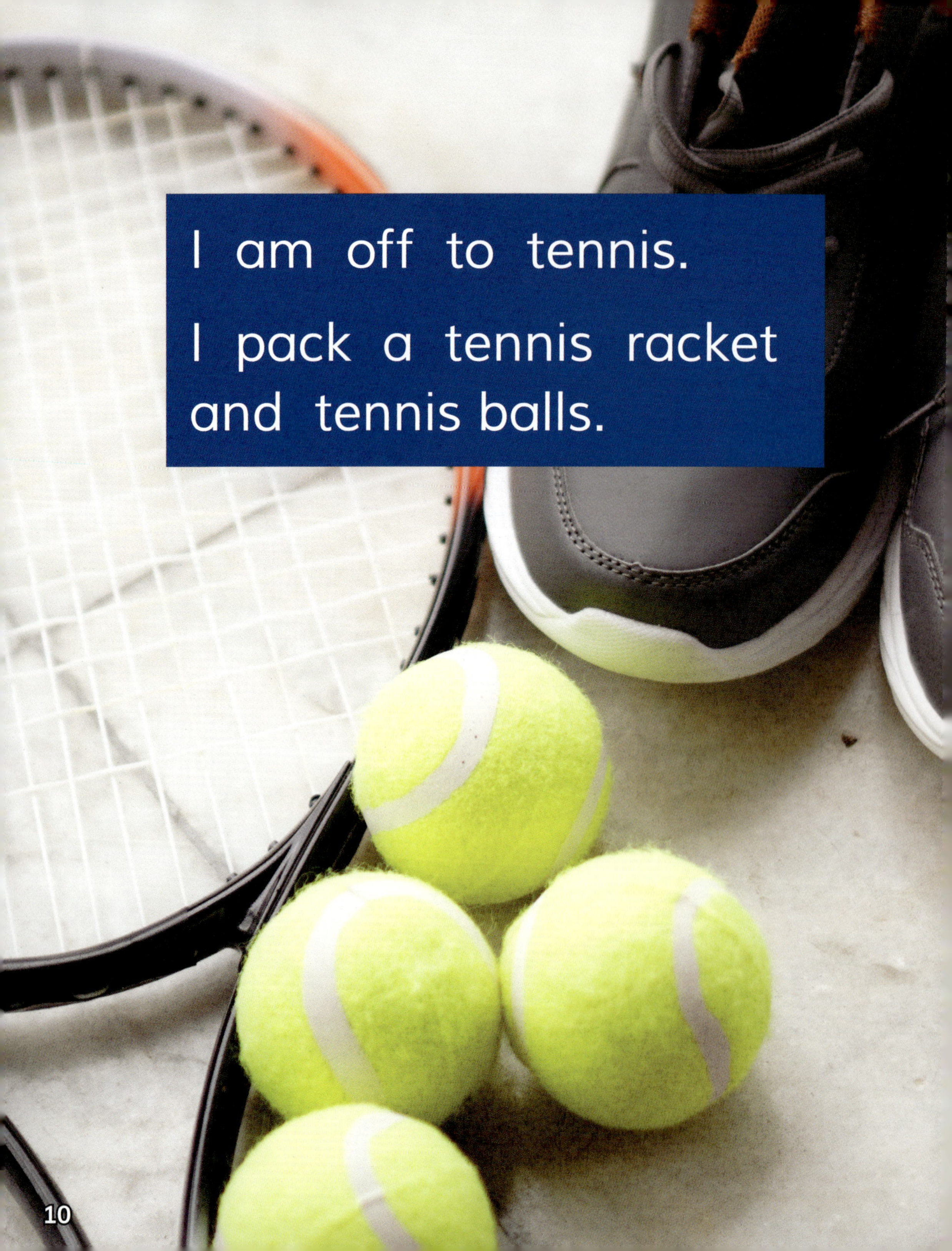

I am off to tennis.
I pack a tennis racket and tennis balls.

At tennis, I pick Ben.
It is **on**!

Ben hit it, but I am fit.

I can run and hit it back to him.

Ben got it, but is it in? No! It is not in.

Ben can huff and
puff, but I got the set.

Can Ben get as hot as I am at tennis?

I reckon Ben can!